Diane Cardano-Casacio

Your Real Estate Consultant For Life

Contents

Foreword

by Joe Stumpf

As a coach who has guided real estate professionals for nearly three decades, I've had the privilege of witnessing countless careers unfold. However, few have impressed and inspired me as much as Diane Cardano-Casacio's journey. Diane isn't just a real estate agent; she's a force of nature, a whirlwind of energy, enthusiasm, and unwavering commitment to excellence.

From the moment Diane joined our By Referral Only community, it was clear she was something special. Her boundless energy, insatiable thirst for knowledge, and relentless pursuit of greatness set her apart. As a full-time member of our BroVance and a valued participant in my Inner Circle, Diane has consistently pushed herself – and those around her – to new heights.

Diane's excellence extends far beyond real estate. She's a world-class athlete, a dedicated golfer, a passionate community advocate, a loving wife to Stan, and a loyal friend to many. In every role she takes on, Diane brings her full self, her best self, to each moment.

In this book, Diane shares the wisdom, strategies, and personal insights that have made her not just a successful real estate professional but a true leader in her field. Let me give you a little preview of what you'll find in these pages:

In Chapter 1, Diane takes you on a nostalgic journey through her childhood, showing how early experiences shaped her unique approach to real estate. Growing up trailing behind her father through model homes, Diane absorbed the essence of real estate from an early age. This foundation inspired her "model home mindset," which became the cornerstone of her success. Her HOMES method, developed to transform expired listings into successful sales, is a testament to her innovative approach.

Chapter 2 delves into the values and principles that form the bedrock of Diane's success. Her FOUNDATION approach emphasizes integrity, resilience, and empathy, building long-term client trust and preparing homes for the market well in advance. Diane's commitment to these core values ensures a solid foundation for her clients' real estate journeys.

In Chapter 3, you'll meet Diane's extraordinary Element Team, where each member embodies an elemental force. Diane's fire drives passion and results, while her team members provide adaptability, positivity, and stability. This elemental synergy creates a balanced and effective team dynamic, harnessing the power of fire, water, sun, and rock to achieve extraordinary results.

Chapter 4 unveils Diane's fierce negotiation strategies that consistently win for her clients. Her CANVAS strategy, which includes creating compelling narratives, analyzing deals, and anticipating objections, secures the best possible outcomes. Diane's approach transforms negotiations into opportunities for success, ensuring her clients come out on top.

In Chapter 5, Diane introduces her innovative Community of Clients approach, transforming traditional real estate transactions into gateways for long-lasting relationships and community building. Her CONNECT method fosters ongoing client relationships, orchestrates opportunities for interaction, and nurtures a supportive client community. Diane's approach creates a sense of belonging that extends far beyond the closing table.

Chapter 6 shares Diane's groundbreaking approach to preparing homes for sale years in advance. Her GARDEN method encourages clients to plant the seeds of a successful sale well before they're ready to list, maximizing value and reducing stress. This proactive strategy ensures that homes are market-ready and positioned for success.

Finally, in Chapter 7, you'll get an inside look at the "Diane-ize Experience." Diane's SYMPHONY method orchestrates every aspect of the real estate journey, delivering exceptional, personalized service that exceeds client expectations. Her approach harmonizes goals with market realities, optimizes property potential, and navigates challenges with grace.

As Diane's coach, I've had the pleasure of watching her implement and refine these strategies over the years. More than that, I've had the joy of watching Diane grow not just as a real estate professional but as a human being. Her commitment to personal growth, her dedication to her clients, and her tireless work ethic are truly inspiring.

This book is more than just a guide to real estate success – it's a testament to what's possible when you combine passion, perseverance, and a genuine desire to improve people's lives. Whether you're a seasoned real estate professional or just starting your career, Diane's insights and experiences will challenge you to think differently, dream bigger, and bring your best self to everything you do.

So, get ready for a journey through the mind of one of the most dynamic, innovative, and inspiring real estate professionals I've ever had the pleasure of coaching. Diane's energy leaps off every page, and I have no doubt that by the time you finish this book, you'll be as impressed and inspired by Diane Cardano as I am.

Welcome to the "Diane-ize Experience." It's going to be one heck of a ride!

Joe Stumpf
Founder, By Referral Only

Overview

Chapter 1. From Model Homes to Real Homes: A Realtor's Origin Story

Ever wonder how a little girl playing in model homes grew up to become the "Expired Listing Queen"? In this chapter, I'll take you on a journey through my childhood, where I unknowingly absorbed the essence of real estate, trailing behind my father through perfectly staged dream homes. You'll discover how these early experiences shaped my unique approach to real estate, instilling in me a "model home mindset" that became the cornerstone of my success. I'll share how I developed my HOMES method, turning challenging expired listings into triumphant sales. Get ready for some heartwarming stories, a few laughs, and insights that'll change the way you think about real estate. This chapter isn't just about my past; it's about unlocking the potential in every home and every client. So, come on in – the door's open, and I can't wait to show you around!

Chapter 2. Building a Foundation: Values and Principles in Real Estate

Ready to dig deep into the bedrock of real estate success? In this chapter, I'm going to let you in on the secret foundation that's supported my entire career. We're talking about more than just business strategies here – we're exploring the core values and principles that can transform your approach to real estate. I'll introduce you to my FOUNDATION approach, a blueprint for building trust and delivering results that stand the test of time. You'll learn how to renovate expectations, not just homes, and discover the power of a client-centered focus. But this isn't just about making sales; it's about creating a legacy that extends far beyond your career. Whether you're a seasoned pro or just starting out, this chapter will challenge you to examine your own foundation and inspire you to build something truly extraordinary. So grab your hard hat – we're about to construct a real estate philosophy that'll weather any market storm!

Chapter 3. The Element Team: Harnessing Fire, Water, Sun and Rock

Imagine a real estate team that embodies the power of the elements themselves. Sounds magical, right? Well, in this chapter, I'm going to introduce you to exactly that. You'll meet my extraordinary Element Team, where each member brings their unique "elemental" energy to create an unbeatable force in real estate. I'm the fire, igniting passion and driving results. Jackie, my buyer's agent, flows like water, adapting to every situation. Bobby radiates positivity like the sun, while my husband Stan provides the rock-solid foundation of wisdom and experience.

And let's not forget our invaluable virtual assistants from the Philippines – while it's night there, they work tirelessly under the stars, shining brightly to handle all the details behind the scenes. Their dedication during their nighttime allows us to shine during our daytime, making us the best elements we can be.

But this isn't just about us – it's about how this elemental approach can transform your real estate experience. You'll discover how we synergize our strengths to overcome any challenge and exceed every expectation. By the end of this chapter, you'll see how the power of a truly balanced team can turn your real estate dreams into reality. So, are you ready to harness the elements and revolutionize your approach to buying or selling? Let's dive in!

Chapter 4. Winning for Clients: Negotiation Strategies of a Fierce Competitor

Buckle up because, in this chapter, we're diving into the thrilling world of real estate negotiations! I'm going to show you how I turn every deal into a masterpiece, using my CANVAS strategy to craft winning outcomes for my clients. You'll learn how to create compelling narratives that resonate with buyers and sellers, analyze deals from every angle, and navigate the emotional turbulence of high-stakes negotiations. But we're not just talking theory here – I'll share real-world examples of how these strategies have helped my clients come out on top, even in the most challenging situations. You'll discover the power of my WIN-WIN-WIN approach, where everyone walks away feeling like a champion. Whether you're a first-time homebuyer or a seasoned investor, this chapter will arm you with the negotiation skills you need to succeed in any real estate market. Ready to become a negotiation ninja? Let's get started!

Chapter 5. Beyond the Transaction: Creating a Community of Clients

In this chapter, I introduce my innovative Community of Clients approach, which transforms the traditional real estate transaction into a gateway for long-lasting relationships and community building. It's called the CONNECT method, which emphasizes the ongoing cultivation of client relationships, orchestrating opportunities for client interactions, nurturing a network of trusted professionals, navigating life changes with expert guidance, educating and empowering clients, creating memorable experiences, and transforming transactions into lifelong connections.

Here, I share real-life examples of how this approach benefits clients, from surprise gifts that show personal attention to community events that foster friendships among neighbors. I discuss my semi-annual "Neighbor Movie Nights," annual events like the "Thanksgiving Pie Open House," and the "Curb Appeal Challenge," all designed to create a sense of belonging among her client community.

The chapter also introduces the LEGACY approach, underscoring my commitment to long-term thinking, engaged community building, genuine care for clients' wellbeing, active support through all life stages, continuous learning and knowledge sharing, and yielding connections that enrich lives for years to come. Ultimately, I paint a picture of a real estate experience that goes far beyond buying or selling a home. It's about becoming part of a supportive, vibrant community that adds value to client's lives long after the transaction is complete, transforming the role of a realtor from a one-time service provider to a trusted, lifelong advisor and friend.

Chapter 6. Preparation Meets Opportunity: Starting the Home Sale Process Early

Ever heard the saying, "The best time to plant a tree was 20 years ago. The second best time is now"? Well, in this chapter, I'm going to show you how this wisdom applies to selling your home. You'll discover my GARDEN method for cultivating your home's potential years before you're ready to sell. I'll share strategies for gauging market trends, making strategic improvements, and documenting your home's journey to create a powerful selling story. You'll learn about my "Slow Burn Renovation" strategy that can transform your home without breaking the bank or disrupting your life. But this isn't just about preparing for a future sale – it's about enhancing your living experience right now while building equity and reducing stress when you eventually decide to sell. By the end of this chapter, you'll have a clear roadmap for turning your home into a market-ready masterpiece, no matter how far off your sale might be. Ready to plant the seeds of your future real estate success? Let's dig in!

Chapter 7. The Diane-sized Experience: Unique Approaches to Exceed Expectations

Get ready for a real estate experience that's anything but ordinary! In this chapter, I'm pulling back the curtain on what I call the "Diane-ize Experience" – a symphony of personalized service, innovative solutions, and exceptional results. You'll discover my SYMPHONY method for orchestrating every aspect of your real estate journey, from synchronizing perfect timing to yielding maximum value. I'll share stories of how this approach has transformed challenges into triumphs for my clients, turning "ugly duckling" houses into sought-after properties and navigating complex deals with grace under pressure. You'll learn about my ENCORE principle, which ensures that every interaction exceeds expectations and creates memorable moments. Whether you're buying, selling, or investing, this chapter will show you how a truly personalized, innovative approach can elevate your real estate dreams to new heights. Ready for a standing-ovation-worthy real estate experience? Let's raise the curtain on your Diane-ize adventure!

Chapter One

From Model Homes to Real Homes

A Realtor's Origin Story

As a child, I never imagined that my playground would become my profession. But looking back, it's clear that real estate was in my DNA from the very beginning. Growing up as the youngest of four children, I was often found trailing behind my father, a successful custom home builder, as he navigated through pristine model homes. These weren't just houses; they were perfectly staged dreams, each one a canvas painted with the promise of a new life.

I can still picture those model homes vividly - the strategically placed furniture, the artfully arranged accessories, and that singular negligee hanging in the closet, a silent suggestion of the life that could be lived within these walls. Everything was painted in harmonious colors, the garage and basement gleaming with fresh coats, though the latter remained unfinished, leaving room for the new owners' imagination to run wild.

Little did I know that these childhood excursions were laying the foundation for my future career. At just five years old, I found myself instinctively guiding potential buyers through these sample homes, pointing out features with the confidence of a seasoned professional. It was as if I was absorbing the essence of real estate through osmosis, each visit adding another layer to my understanding of what makes a house truly sellable.

The Model Home Mindset: Building Dreams One Room at a Time

As I grew older, my fascination with these perfectly curated spaces only intensified. I began to see beyond the surface-level aesthetics, understanding the psychology behind each design choice. The model home wasn't just a structure; it was a storytelling device, a three-dimensional narrative that invited potential buyers to envision their own happily ever after.

This "model home mindset" would become the cornerstone of my approach to real estate. It taught me that selling a home isn't just about square footage and floor plans; it's about painting a picture of possibility, of helping clients see the potential in every space, no matter how humble or lived-in it might be.

When I finally entered the real estate world at 33, armed with my MBA in marketing and years of unconscious training, I found myself uniquely equipped to tackle one of the industry's most challenging niches: expired listings. These were the homes that other agents had failed to sell, properties that had languished on the market, their owners growing increasingly frustrated and disillusioned.

But where others saw failure, I saw opportunity. With each expired listing, I walked through the door, armed with the vision of that perfect model home from my childhood. I could instantly see what needed to be done - a fresh coat of paint here, a decluttered space there, a strategic rearrangement of furniture to maximize flow and appeal. It was as if I had a superpower, the ability to transform lived-in spaces into showcases of potential.

The HOMES Approach: Turning Failures into Triumphs

My success with expired listings wasn't just luck or innate talent. It was the result of a systematic approach I developed, which I like to call the **HOMES Method:**

H - Honest assessment of the property's strengths and weaknesses

O - Optimized staging to highlight the home's best features

M - Market analysis to ensure competitive pricing

E - Effective marketing to reach the right buyers

S - Strategic negotiations to close the deal

This approach allowed me to breathe new life into properties that others had given up on. I became known as the "Expired Listing Queen," a title I wore with pride. It wasn't just about making sales; it was about restoring hope to sellers who had begun to believe their homes were unsellable.

The Art of the Turnaround: From Stagnant to Sold

One particularly memorable case involved a charming colonial that had been on the market for over a year. The owners were at their wits' end, having cycled through three different agents with no success. When I first walked through the door, I could immediately see why the house hadn't sold - it was stuck in a time warp, with dated wallpaper and cluttered rooms that made the space feel small and uninviting.

But beneath the surface, I could see the bones of a beautiful home. Using my HOMES approach, I worked with the sellers to make strategic updates. We stripped away the wallpaper, painted the walls in neutral, inviting tones, and decluttered ruthlessly. I brought in some key staging pieces to highlight the home's best features and create a sense of flow between rooms.

The transformation was remarkable. What was once a tired, overlooked property became the talk of the neighborhood. We relisted the home on a Friday, and by Monday, we had multiple offers above the asking price. The sellers, who had been close to giving up hope, were overjoyed.

This experience reinforced a crucial lesson: in real estate, perception is everything. My job wasn't just to list homes; it was to reimagine them, to help both sellers and buyers see the potential that lay hidden beneath years of lived-in comfort.

From Accidental Agent to Intentional Expert

While my childhood experiences laid the groundwork for my real estate career, my entry into the profession wasn't exactly planned. After a stint in corporate America and a foray into multi-level marketing (selling water filters, of all things), I found myself at a crossroads. It was during this time of uncertainty that a chance encounter at the gym changed the course of my life.

Stan, who would later become my husband, suggested I consider real estate. At first, I balked at the idea of working weekends, preferring to spend that time with friends. But the seed had been planted, and the more I thought about it, the more it made sense. Real estate wasn't just a job; it was a calling that had been whispering to me my entire life.

The REALTOR Mindset: More Than Just a Career Choice

As I embraced my new path, I realized that being a realtor wasn't just about selling houses; it was about embodying a set of values and principles that would guide every interaction and decision. I developed what I call the **REALTOR Mindset:**

R - Resilience in the face of challenges

E - Empathy for clients' needs and emotions

A - Adaptability to changing market conditions

L - Leadership in guiding clients through complex transactions

T - Tenacity in pursuing the best outcomes

O - Optimism about finding the perfect solution

R - Responsibility to always act in the client's best interest

This mindset became my North Star, guiding me through the ups and downs of the real estate market. It helped me weather the storm of the 2008 recession, a pivotal moment that forced me to innovate and adapt.

Seminars and Systems: Planting Seeds for Future Success

As the housing market took a hit in 2008, I knew I had to do something to stay ahead of the curve. That's when I had the idea to start hosting home seller seminars. These weren't just about immediate sales; they were about building a pool of future clients, educating them on the intricacies of the real estate market, and positioning myself as a trusted advisor long before they were ready to list their homes.

These seminars became a cornerstone of my business strategy. I would go to people's homes a year, sometimes even five years, before they were planning to sell. I'd offer free "room-by-room reviews," pointing out areas for improvement and helping them create a long-term plan to maximize their home's value.

This approach had multiple benefits. For the homeowners, it took much of the stress out of the selling process. They could make improvements gradually, on their own timeline, rather than rushing to get everything done in the weeks before listing. For me, it created a pipeline of loyal clients who trusted my expertise and were primed for success when they finally decided to sell.

The Power of Preparation: Winning Before the Game Begins

My seminar strategy was built on a simple principle: the best time to prepare for selling a home is long before you're ready to list. This approach allowed me to help clients in ways that went far beyond the typical realtor-client relationship. We could strategically time renovations and updates, taking advantage of seasonal lulls in contractor demand to get better prices. We could take exterior photos when the landscaping was at its best, ensuring we had stunning imagery ready to go, regardless of when the house actually hit the market.

This level of preparation and attention to detail gave my clients a significant advantage. When their homes finally went on the market, they weren't just ready - they were primed to outshine the competition. It was like we were playing chess while everyone else was playing checkers.

The result? Homes that sold faster and for higher prices than the neighborhood average. Clients who felt confident and in control throughout the process. And a reputation for excellence that led to a steady stream of referrals and repeat business.

The Model Home Mindset in Action

As I reflect on my journey from that wide-eyed five-year-old in model homes to the "Expired Listing Queen" and beyond, I'm struck by how those early experiences shaped my entire approach to real estate. The model home mindset - the ability to see the potential in every space and to help others see it, too - has been the thread that ties my entire career together.

It's a mindset that's about more than just selling houses. It's about helping people transition from one chapter of their lives to the next. It's about turning houses into homes and dreams into reality. It's about approaching each client and each property with the same enthusiasm and attention to detail that I had when I was first exploring those perfectly staged model homes.

In the chapters that follow, I'll delve deeper into the strategies, experiences, and lessons that have defined my career in real estate. From navigating market downturns to embracing new technologies, from building a stellar team to creating a community of clients, each chapter will offer insights and practical advice for anyone looking to succeed in the dynamic world of real estate.

But at the heart of it all is that little girl who fell in love with the magic of model homes. She taught me that with the right vision, any house can become a showcase of potential, and any challenge can become an opportunity for growth and success. That's the true essence of the model home mindset - and it's a lesson I carry with me every day.

Chapter Two

Building a Foundation

Values and Principles in Real Estate

I know that my approach to real estate is different. It's not just about selling houses; it's about building a foundation of trust, integrity, and results that will stand the test of time. Like the custom homes my father built, I want my career to be constructed on solid ground, with each transaction adding another brick to a legacy of excellence that benefits you, my client.

The Blueprint of Success: Values as Cornerstones

In real estate, as in life, your values are the cornerstones upon which everything else is built. For me, these cornerstones were laid early, shaped by my experiences as the youngest of four in a family where hard work and integrity were prized above all else. I watched my father pour his heart and soul into every home he built, and I bring that same level of commitment to you.

My core values are the blueprint for my business:

1. Integrity: Always doing what's right for you, even when no one is watching.

2. Resilience: Bouncing back from setbacks stronger than before, ensuring your journey is smooth.

3. Innovation: Constantly seeking new ways to serve you better.

4. Empathy: Truly understanding and addressing your needs and fears.

5. Excellence: Never settle for "good enough" when greatness is possible for you.

To put these values into action for you, I've developed what I call the **FOUNDATION Approach:**

F - Focus on your needs above all else

O - Open communication with you at every step of the process

U - Understand the emotional aspects of your buying and selling journey

N - Never stop learning and improving to serve you better

D - Deliver results that exceed your expectations

A - Adapt to changing market conditions to protect your interests

T - Take responsibility for both successes and failures in your transactions

I - Innovate constantly to stay ahead of the curve for you

O - Offer solutions, not just listings, to meet your unique needs

N - Nurture a long-term relationship with you beyond the transaction

This approach is the scaffolding upon which I build my service to you. It's not just about closing deals; it's about creating a structure of trust and expertise that will support you through one of the most significant transactions of your life.

Framing the Future: The Power of Preparation for You

One of the key principles that sets my approach apart is the emphasis on preparation for you. I've learned that the best time to start preparing your home for sale is long before the "For Sale" sign goes up in your yard. This principle becomes the frame around which I build my unique seminar strategy for you.

By offering you free room-by-room reviews and long-term planning sessions, I help you see your home through the eyes of potential buyers. We walk through each space together, identifying areas for improvement and creating a roadmap for maximizing your home's value. This isn't just about quick fixes; it's about strategic enhancements that will pay dividends when it comes time for you to sell.

For you, this approach is a game-changer. Instead of feeling overwhelmed by a long list of repairs and updates in the weeks before listing, you can tackle projects gradually, on your own timeline. This not only reduces your stress but often results in significant cost savings for you. By planning ahead, we can take advantage of seasonal lulls in contractor demand, negotiating better rates and ensuring higher quality work for your home.

The benefits of this approach for you are manifold:

1. You feel more in control of the selling process.

2. Your home is better prepared to stand out in a competitive market.

3. We time improvements to maximize your return on investment.

4. The actual listing process becomes smoother and less stressful for you.

5. Your home often sells faster and for a higher price than comparable properties.

This principle of preparation extends beyond just physical improvements. I encourage you to start decluttering early, to begin the emotional process of detaching from your home, and to think critically about your next move. By the time we're ready to list, you're not just prepared; you're primed for success.

The Architecture of Trust: Building a Lasting Relationship with You

In real estate, trust is the mortar that holds everything together. Without it, even the most beautifully staged home or the most competitive offer can crumble. That's why I make building trust with you the centerpiece of my business model.

Trust, I've learned, isn't something I can demand or expect from you. It's something I earn, brick by brick, through consistent actions and unwavering integrity. I build it in the small moments - returning your call promptly, remembering your preferences, and going the extra mile for you even when it's inconvenient. And I cement it in the big moments - negotiating fiercely on your behalf, being honest with you even when it's difficult, and always, always putting your needs first.

The result is a level of trust that goes beyond the typical agent-client relationship. You don't just see me as your realtor; you see me as a trusted advisor, a friend, and a partner in your journey. This trust becomes the foundation for a long-term relationship that lasts well beyond the closing table.

Renovating Expectations: The Art of Exceeding Your Expectations

In a world where overpromising and underdelivering have become all too common, I make it my mission to do the opposite for you. Like a skilled renovator who transforms a fixer-upper into a dream home, I seek to renovate your expectations of what a realtor can do for you.

This means going above and beyond for you in ways both big and small:

- Providing a moving truck for you if you need help decluttering or moving

- Offering you a line of credit to cover improvement costs before selling

- Creating detailed, room-by-room improvement plans for your home

- Leveraging my network of contractors to get you the best rates on renovations

- Hosting seminars and workshops to educate you on market trends and homeimprovement strategies

Each of these services is designed not just to help sell your home but to make the entire process easier and more rewarding for you. By consistently delivering more than I promise, I build a relationship with you that sets me apart in a crowded market.

The Blueprint of Client-Centered Service for You

At the heart of my approach is a simple but powerful principle: everything I do must benefit you, my client. This client-centered focus is the blueprint for every aspect of my service to you. Whether I'm negotiating a deal, staging your home, or simply offering advice, the question I always ask myself is, "How does this serve my client's best interests?"

This approach manifests in several key ways for you:

1. Transparent Communication: I make it a point to explain every step of the process to you in clear, jargon-free language. You never have to wonder what's happening or why.

2. Education-First Mindset: Through seminars, one-on-one consultations, and ongoing communication, I empower you with knowledge. An informed client, I believe, is a confident client.

3. Customized Strategies: Recognizing that no two clients or properties are the same, I tailor my approach to your unique situation. Cookie-cutter solutions have no place in my playbook for you.

4. Long-Term Perspective: I'm not interested in quick sales at the expense of your satisfaction. My goal is to build a relationship with you that will last for years, even decades.

5. Holistic Support: Recognizing that buying or selling a home affects every aspect of your life, I offer support that goes beyond just the trans-action. From recommending schools to suggesting local services, I aim to be a comprehensive resource for you.

This client-centered approach not only leads to better outcomes for you but also results in a steady stream of referrals and repeat business. It's a win-win strategy that aligns perfectly with my values and goals and, most importantly, serves your best interests.

The Foundation of a Legacy: Building More Than Just a Transaction for You

As my career progresses and my reputation grows, I realize that I'm build-ing more than just a successful real estate business. I'm laying the founda-tion for a legacy that extends far beyond my own career, and you're a crucial part of that legacy.

This legacy is built on several key pillars that benefit you:

1. Mentorship: Just as I was guided by the wisdom of my father and others in my early years, I make it a priority to continually improve my skills and knowledge to serve you better.

2. Community Building: Through client events, seminars, and community involvement, I work to create a network of home-owners and professionals that you can tap into for support and learning.

3. Innovation: By constantly seeking new ways to serve you better, I help push the industry forward, setting new standards for what you can expect from your realtor.

4. Ethical Leadership: In an industry sometimes plagued by questionable practices, I stand firm in my commitment to integrity and transparency, ensuring you always receive honest, ethical service.

5. Lasting Relationships: The bond I form with you often lasts long after the transaction is complete. This relationship becomes the true measure of my success.

This legacy-focused approach gives deeper meaning to my work with you. It's not just about selling your home or helping you buy a new one; it's about making a lasting positive impact on your life, your community, and the real estate industry as a whole.

The Unshakeable Foundation of Success for You

As I reflect on the values and principles that guide my career and my service to you, I'm reminded of a quote by Frank Lloyd Wright: "The longer I live, the more beautiful life becomes. If you foolishly ignore beauty, you will soon find yourself without it. Your life will be impoverished. But if you invest in beauty, it will remain with you all the days of your life."

In real estate, as in architecture, beauty is found not just in the final product but in the strength of the foundation, the integrity of the structure, and the vision that brings it all together. By building my career and my relationship with you on a foundation of solid values, unwavering principles, and a genuine commitment to serving you, I create something beautiful that enriches not only my life but your life as well.

This foundation - built on integrity, resilience, innovation, empathy, and excellence - allows me to weather market storms, overcome challenges, and continually reach new heights of success in serving you. It's a foundation that not only supports my own career but provides a stable platform for you to build your dreams upon as well.

As we move forward together, exploring the strategies, experiences, and innovations that shape my approach to your real estate journey, remember that at the core of it all lies this unshakeable foundation. It's a foundation that I build for you, regardless of your experience or background, because I'm committed to values that put you first and to principles that stand the test of time.

In the end, that's what real estate - and indeed, any truly fulfilling career - is all about building something beautiful, something lasting, something that improves your life. And that, more than any sale or commission, is the true measure of my success in serving you.

Chapter Three

The Element Team

Harnessing Fire, Water, Sun and Rock

When I think about what sets my approach apart in the world of real estate, I'm reminded of the ancient elements: fire, water, sun, and rock. Each of these forces of nature plays a crucial role in creating and sustaining life on our planet. In the same way, I've built a team that embodies these elemental powers, working in harmony to create extraordinary experiences for our clients.

Let me take you on a journey through the Cardano Team, where each member brings their unique "elemental" energy to the table, all focused on one goal: helping you, our client, achieve your real estate dreams.

The Fire: Igniting Passion and Drive

In our team, I'm often described as the fire. Like a carefully tended flame, I bring warmth, light, and transformative energy to every transaction. But this fire isn't just about heat and intensity; it's about illumination and transformation.

Imagine you're selling your family home of 30 years. It's filled with memories, cluttered with decades of life, and perhaps a bit outdated. When I walk through that door, I don't just see a house that needs work. I see potential waiting tobe unleashed, a diamond in the rough that needs only the right touch to shine.

My "fire" approach means I'll be honest with you - sometimes brutally so. I might say, "That semi-gloss paint in the living room? It's giving off a bit of a 'ghetto' vibe." But here's the thing: that honesty isn't meant to hurt. It's meant to ignite change, to spark the transformation that will turn your lived-in house into a buyer's dream home.

This fiery passion extends to negotiations, too. When I'm fighting for your interests, I'm relentless. I once had a situation where a buyer's initial offer was $675,000. After some back-and-forth, they lowered it to $625,000 with an escalation clause up to $675,000. Most agents would have been tempted to take that offer. But I saw an opportunity to fan the flames.

I told the buyer's agent their offer was off the table, implying we had better offers (we didn't). The result? They came back with $721,000 and a stronger appraisal guarantee. That's the power of fire - it can forge steel, turning a good deal into a great one.

But here's what you need to understand about fire: it needs fuel to keep burning. In real estate, that fuel is knowledge, preparation, and strategic thinking. That's why I'm constantly feeding the flames, staying up-to-date on market trends, attending mastermind groups with top agents across the country, and always looking for innovative ways to serve my clients better.

For you, this means you're not just getting an agent; you're getting a fierce advocate armed with the latest industry insights and strategies. Whether you're buying or selling, I'm bringing that fire to every aspect of your transaction, illuminating the path to success and burning through obstacles that stand in our way.

The Water: Flowing with Adaptability and Nurture

While I bring the fire, my buyer's agent, Jackie, embodies the element of water. Like a river that finds its way around every obstacle, Jackie's adaptability and nurturing nature make her an invaluable asset to our team and to you, our client.

Let me tell you about Sarah and Mike, a young couple who came to us frustrated after months of unsuccessful house hunting with another agent. Sarah, an avid reader, dreamed of cozy nooks for her books. Mike, a hobbyist woodworker, longed for a spacious workshop. Their previous agent had been showing them cookie-cutter homes that left them feeling unfulfilled.

Enter Jackie with her water-like ability to flow with the currents of their desires. On their first outing, she noticed Sarah's eyes light up at a built-in bookshelf while Mike lingered in a roomy garage. Jackie didn't just hear their words; she sensed the undercurrents of their needs.

As they visited more homes, Jackie's warmth melted away their frustrations. She encouraged open conversations, creating a safe space for Sarah and Mike to explore their true wants. When budget concerns arose, Jackie didn't push or pull. Instead, she gently guided them toward unexplored neighborhoods that offered great value.

Two weeks into their search, Jackie brought them to a charming craftsman home. Sarah gasped at the living room's floor-to-ceiling bookshelves while Mike's eyes widened at the detached garage perfect for his woodworking. It was a home they hadn't even realized they were looking for until Jackie's intuitive understanding led them there.

Throughout the buying process, Jackie's flexibility shone through. When the inspection revealed minor issues, she calmly negotiated with the sellers, securing necessary repairs without ruffling feathers. Her openness to creative solutions smoothed every bump in the road.

By the time Sarah and Mike moved in, they felt they'd not only found their dream home but gained a friend. Jackie's water-like qualities – her flexibility, deep listening, openness to possibilities, and warmth – had carried them effortlessly to their goal, transforming a potentially stressful process into a joyful journey of discovery.

The Sun: Illuminating Possibilities and Fostering Growth

Every successful team needs a constant source of energy and optimism. For us, that's my nephew Bobby. He's our sun, radiating warmth, consistency, and illuminating potential in every situation.

Let me share a story that perfectly captures Bobby's solar energy. We were working with the Johnsons, a family selling their home of 2 years. The house was outdated, cluttered, and in need of serious TLC. The Johnsons were overwhelmed, ready to accept a low offer just to be done with the process.

That's when Bobby stepped in, his enthusiasm as bright as the summer sun. He didn't see a hopeless case; he saw a golden opportunity. With boundless energy, he rolled up his sleeves and got to work. He organized a team of contractors, coordinated repairs, and even pitched in himself, painting walls and landscaping the overgrown yard.

Throughout the process, Bobby's optimism was unwavering. When Mrs. Johnson worried about the cost of updates, Bobby helped her see how each improvement would yield returns. When Mr. Johnson felt nostalgic about parting with old furniture, Bobby suggested ways to honor those memories while creating a more appealing space for buyers.

Bobby's innovative thinking turned challenges into opportunities. He transformed the cluttered basement into a chic home office, appealing to remote workers. The overgrown backyard became a charming cottage garden, a selling point for nature lovers.

His energy was contagious. Soon, the Johnsons were excited about the transformation, eagerly participating in the process. Bobby's steady presence kept them motivated, and his helpful attitude solved problems as they arose.

When the home hit the market, it was barely recognizable. Light streamed through freshly washed windows, highlighting the home's beautiful bones. The open house was a smash hit, with multiple offers coming in well above the asking price.

But Bobby's sun-like qualities shone brightest when a last-minute hiccup threatened to derail the sale. The buyers' financing fell through just days before closing. While others might have panicked, Bobby remained a beacon of calm optimism. He worked tirelessly, leveraging his network to find a solution. Within 48 hours, he'd connected the buyers with a lender who could expedite the process, saving the deal.

Through it all, Bobby's energy never dimmed. His steadfast presence, helpful attitude, innovative thinking, never-ending optimism, and energetic approach turned what could have been a challenging sale into a resounding success. The Johnsons not only sold their home for top dollar but also gained a new appreciation for the potential that had been hiding in their beloved family home all along.

The Rock: Providing Stability and Wisdom

Every successful real estate transaction needs a solid foundation, a source of stability and wisdom that can weather any storm. In our team, that's my husband, Stan. He's our rock, providing the grounding force that keeps us steady and the deep knowledge that helps us navigate even the most complex situations.

Let me tell you about the Allens, a couple looking to buy their forever home. They'd found a beautiful Victorian-era house full of character and charm. But beneath that charm lurked potential issues that could turn their dream into a nightmare.

Enter Stan, our team's bedrock. When the Allens expressed concerns about the home's age, Stan didn't dismiss their worries. Instead, he approached the situation with the balanced perspective of someone who's seen it all.

He arranged for a comprehensive inspection, going beyond the basics to check for hidden issues common in older homes.

The inspection revealed significant problems: outdated wiring, a crumbling foundation, and a roof on its last legs. Many buyers would have walked away, but Stan saw an opportunity to create something truly special.

With his extensive knowledge of construction and real estate, Stan broke down the issues for the Allens. He explained each problem in detail, outlining potential solutions and their costs. His calm presence during these discussions kept the Allens grounded, preventing them from making decisions based on emotion rather than fact.

Stan's reasoned approach to problem-solving came to the fore as he developed a comprehensive renovation plan. He brought in trusted contractors, negotiated fair prices, and created a timeline that would transform the house without breaking the bank.

When negotiations with the seller got heated over who should bear the cost of repairs, Stan's dependability shone through. He stood firm, backing up his arguments with data and market insights. His objective analysis of the home's value, considering both its current state and its potential, gave the Allens confidence in their position.

Throughout the process, Stan's keen insight into market trends and property values proved invaluable. He helped the Allens understand how their investment in renovations would pay off in the long run, both in terms of property value and quality of life.

Even when unexpected issues arose during renovations - as they often do with older homes - Stan remained a calm presence. His vast experience meant he always had a Plan B (and often a Plan C and D) ready to go.

By the time the renovations were complete, the Allens had more than just a house - they had a meticulously restored piece of history, updated for modern living while retaining its original charm. And they had the peace of mind that comes from knowing their home was built on a solid foundation, both literally and figuratively.

Stan's rock-solid qualities - his balanced perspective, extensive knowledge, dependability, reasoned approach, objective analysis, calm presence, and keen insight - had turned a potentially risky purchase into a sound investment and a true dream home.

The Stars That Shine On Us

The Elemental Synergy: How It AllComes Together for You

Now, you might be wondering, "This all sounds great, but how does it actually benefit me?" Let me paint you a picture of how our elemental team works together to create an extraordinary experience for you.

Imagine you're the Thompsons, a growing family looking to upgrade from your starter home to a space that can accommodate your expanding needs. You're selling your current home and buying a new one simultaneously - a notoriously stressful and complex process. Here's how our team's elemental synergy works for you:

As your journey begins, I bring my fire energy, igniting your vision for what's possible. We walk through your current home, and I don't hold back. "That popcorn ceiling? It's got to go," I say, already envisioning the smooth,modern finish that will appeal to buyers. My passion ignites your own, and soon, you're seeing your home through new eyes, ready to make the changes that will maximize its value.

Meanwhile, Jackie flows in with her water energy. She listens deeply as you describe your dream home - the open kitchen for family gatherings, the backyard for summer barbecues, and the home office for remote work. She intuits needs you haven't even voiced, like the importance of good schools for your kids' future. Her adaptability shines as she adjusts the home search based on your evolving wishes, always keeping you in the loop and never making you feel pressured.

As the process unfolds, challenges inevitably arise. The buyers for your current home are being difficult, nitpicking every detail. The perfect new home you found needs some work before you can move in. This is where Bobby's solar energy becomes crucial. He shines his unwavering optimism on every situation, keeping you motivated when stress threatens to overwhelm you. His innovative thinking turns problems into opportunities - that difficult buyer? Bobby suggests sweetening the deal with some of your furniture, solving their concerns, and making your move easier in one stroke.

Throughout it all, Stan provides the rock-solid foundation you need. When you're uncertain about taking on a fixer-upper, Stan's deep knowledge of construction reassures you. He breaks down the renovation process, explaining how each improvement will add value to your new home. His calm presence during negotiations ensures you get the best deal on both the sale of your old home and the purchase of the new one.

Lastly, I cannot forget our hard-working Filipino ladies. Our Virtual Assistants from the Philippines are integral to our real estate team's success. They handle all the essential paperwork, ensuring that every detail is meticulously managed, which allows us to focus on client interactions and strategy. They also monitor emails, keeping communication seamless and ensuring that no inquiry goes unanswered. In the often complex process of buying and selling homes, their support is invaluable—they ease the process by being constantly available on WhatsApp, fielding our client's questions, and providing timely responses even when we're not immediately available.

Their role extends beyond administrative tasks; they increase our team's overall communication efficiency, ensuring that clients feel supported at all times. Whether it's tracking us down during an emergency or helping a client after hours, they are the unsung heroes who keep everything running smoothly. Always working hard, they shine brightly over us, smiling as they perform their tasks with dedication and excellence.

This elemental synergy creates a real estate experience that's not just successful but transformative. You're not just selling a house and buying another; you're being guided through a journey of change and growth, supported by a team that brings the power of the elements to every aspect of your transaction.

Our approach is more than just a strategy; it's a promise to you. It's a promise of expertise in every aspect of your real estate journey, from market analysis to home staging to contract negotiation. It's a pledge of unwavering loyalty to your interests, always putting your needs first. We bring an energy that drives results, pushing through obstacles and seizing opportunities on your behalf.

Our motivation to exceed your expectations means we're not satisfied until you're thrilled with the outcome. We approach your unique situation with empathy, understanding that buying or selling a home is not just a financial transaction but an emotional journey. Our negotiation skills secure the best deals, whether you're buying or selling. We leverage our collective strengths through teamwork, ensuring you benefit from our combined centuries of real estate experience.

And our support goes beyond the closing table. Long after the papers are signed, we're here for you, ready to offer advice on home maintenance, connect you with trusted contractors, or simply celebrate your home anniversaries with you.

This is the Cardano Team difference. We bring the power of the elements and support of our Virtual Assistants - the transformative energy of fire, the nurturing flow of water, the illuminating warmth of the sun, and the solid dependability of rock - to every client, every transaction, every time. It's not just about buying or selling a home; it's about creating an extraordinary real estate experience that sets the foundation for the next chapter of your life.

As we embark on your real estate journey together, remember that you have the power of the elements on your side. Together, we'll ignite your vision, flow through challenges, illuminate possibilities, and build on a foundation of rock-solid expertise. That's our promise to you.

Chapter Four

Winning for Clients

Negotiation Strategies of a Fierce Competitor

When I step into a negotiation, I'm not just representing my clients; I'm fighting for their dreams. It's like I'm stepping into the ring, but instead of boxing gloves, I'm armed with market knowledge, psychological insights, and a relentless drive to win. This isn't just business for me—it's personal. Every client's victory is my victory, and I'll go to the mat to make sure we come out on top.

The Art of the Deal: Painting a Masterpiece of Negotiation

Imagine negotiation as a blank canvas. Most agents see it as a simple picture—offer, counteroffer, done. But I see it as an opportunity to create a masterpiece. Every brushstroke matters, from the initial price positioning to the final signature on the closing documents.

Let me give you an example. Recently, I had a client named Loretta. She was an older woman who could not do the steps anymore. Her husband passed away, and It was finally time to move to independent living close to her daughter and her family. A local real estate agent found out that Loretta was going to put her home on the market. He walked through with his buyer, and he told her his buyer was willing to pay $620,000 for her home. She was thrilled with that offer; however, she called me as she did not trust the agent and wanted me to handle the negotiations. I came over and said we could get more than $620,000! I advised her to hold off and let me do four staging repairs to the home and then go on the market priced at $649,999. We went on the market on a Saturday, and I let the weekend play out. Sure enough, on Monday, we had multiple offers, and I was able to leverage them against each other.

The initial buyer came back with a cash offer of $650,000 with an escalation clause of up to $680,000. Here's where the artistry comes in. Another offer came in at $700,000. I did not take this higher offer. I painted a picture of urgency and competition for the initial buyer and their agent with the $680,000 offer. I hinted that I had higher offers (which, truthfully, we did; however, we did not want to take it; they were getting a mortgage, and they wanted a long settlement date.) The result? The initial buyer came back with a staggering $720,000 cash offer, $100,000 over their initial offer, and $70,000 over the asking price.

This isn't just luck or aggressive tactics. It's about understanding the psychology of buyers and sellers, reading the market like a book, and knowing when to push and when to hold back. It's about creating a masterpiece where everyone feels like they've won.

The CANVAS Strategy: Crafting Winning Negotiations

To help my clients understand my approach to negotiations, I've developed what I call the **CANVAS Strategy:**

C - Create a compelling narrative

A - Analyze all angles of the deal

N - Navigate emotional turbulence

V - Value-add beyond the price

A - Anticipate and prepare for objections

S - Secure the best possible outcome

Let's break this down and see how it benefits you, whether you're buying or selling.

Creating a Compelling Narrative

Every home has a story, and every buyer and seller has a dream. My job is to weave these together into a narrative that resonates emotionally and logically. For sellers, this might mean highlighting how your home's unique features align perfectly with what buyers in the market are seeking. For buyers, it's about painting a picture of how this home fits into your life story.

I remember working with a young couple buying their first home. They were outbid on several properties and were getting discouraged. When we found a home they loved, I didn't just submit an offer. I crafted a letter that told their story—how they met volunteering at a local animal shelter, their dreams of starting a family, and their commitment to the community. This narrative, combined with a solid offer, won them the house over higher bids.

Analyzing All Angles of the Deal

In negotiations, knowledge is power. I don't just look at comparable sales and market trends. I dive deep into every aspect of the deal. What's motivating the other party? What are their time constraints? Are there any hidden opportunities or pitfalls?

This comprehensive analysis allows me to find leverage points that others might miss. For instance, I once represented a seller who was frustrated by low offers on their home. By digging deeper, I discovered that the local zoning laws were about to change, making the property much more valuable for development. Armed with this knowledge, we were able to attract a different set of buyers and ultimately sold for well above the initial asking price.

Navigating Emotional Turbulence

Real estate transactions are inherently emotional. People aren't just buying or selling a house; they're making a major life change. My role is often part realtor and part therapist, helping clients navigate the emotional ups and downs of the process.

I had a client who was selling her childhood home after her parents passed away. Every offer felt like an emotional blow to her. I took the time to listen to her stories about the house, to honor her memories, and to help her see how selling the home could be a positive step in her healing process. By addressing the emotional aspect, we were able to negotiate more effectively and ultimately found a buyer who appreciated the home's history as much as she did.

Value-Add Beyond the Price

In a competitive market, sometimes the highest offer isn't the best offer. I train my clients to look beyond the numbers and consider the entire package. This might mean a faster closing, a rent-back agreement, or waived contingencies.

For buyers, I often find creative ways to make their offers stand out. I once had a client who was competing for a home against several all-cash offers. Instead of just increasing the price, we offered to let the sellers stay in the home rent-free for two months after closing, giving them time to find their next home. This unique value-add won us the deal, even though we weren't the highest bidder.

Anticipating and Preparing for Objections

In negotiations, surprises can be costly. That's why I spend considerable time anticipating potential objections or roadblocks and preparing responses in advance. This proactive approach often allows us to address concerns before they become deal-breakers.

For example, when listing a home, I recommend pre-listing inspections. This allows us to identify and address any issues upfront, removing potential negotiation points for buyers. It also demonstrates transparency and builds trust, often leading to smoother negotiations and higher offers.

Securing the Best Possible Outcome

At the end of the day, my goal is simple: to secure the best possible outcome for my clients. This doesn't always mean the highest price for sellers or the lowest price for buyers. It means achieving a result that aligns with your specific goals and circumstances.

I once worked with a seller who prioritized a quick, hassle-free sale over maximizing profit. By understanding this, we were able to price the home strategically, attract multiple offers quickly, and close with a buyer who was willing to accommodate a flexible move-out date. The sale price was slightly below what we might have gotten with a longer marketing period, but the smooth, rapid transaction was exactly what my client needed.

The WIN-WIN-WIN Approach: Where Everyone Comes Out Ahead

Now, you might be thinking, "This all sounds great to me, but what about the other side of the transaction?" This is where my **WIN-WIN-WIN Approach** comes in. I believe that the best negotiations result in all parties feeling satisfied with the outcome. Here's how it breaks down:

W - We (the client) get what we need

I - Integrity is maintained throughout the process

N - Negotiation leads to mutual satisfaction

W - Win for the other party, too

I - Innovative solutions are found

N - New relationships are built

W - Wider community benefits

I - Industry standards are elevated

N - Next transaction is made easier

This approach isn't just a feel-good philosophy; it's smart business. When everyone walks away feeling good about the deal, it leads to smoother transactions, positive referrals, and a reputation that opens doors for future negotiations.

Let me give you a real-world example. I once represented a seller in a multiple-offer situation. We had several strong offers, but one stood out—not because it was the highest, but because the buyers had written a heartfelt letter about how much they loved the neighborhood and wanted to raise their family there.

My seller was torn. The highest offer was from an investor who planned to rent out the property. The family's offer was strong but about $10,000 lower. Instead of just pushing for the highest price, I suggested a compromise. We countered the family's offer, asking them to match the highest bid. In return, we offered to leave behind some high-end appliances that the seller had initially planned to take.

The result? The family stretched to meet the price, the seller got their desired number and felt good about passing their beloved home to a young family, and the buyers got a move-in ready home with premium appliances. That's a WIN-WIN-WIN.

This approach has long-term benefits, too. The happy buyers have referred multiple friends to me. The seller called me years later to help them buy their retirement home. And the positive energy from that transaction has rippled out into the community, enhancing my reputation and making future negotiations easier.

The NEGOTIATE Mindset: Your Secret Weapon in Any Transaction

To help my clients internalize this winning approach to negotiations, I've developed what I call the **NEGOTIATE Mindset:**

N - Never settle for less than your worth

E - Empathize with the other party's position

G - Go beyond the obvious in seeking solutions

O - Open communication channels and keep them flowing

T - Time the market and your moves strategically

I - Invest in preparation and knowledge

A - Always maintain integrity

T - Think long-term relationships, not just short-term gains

E - Elevate the entire process through professionalism

Adopting this mindset doesn't just help you win negotiations; it transforms the entire real estate experience. Instead of a stressful, adversarial process, it becomes an opportunity for growth, connection, and mutual benefit.

For you, my client, this means peace of mind knowing that you have a fierce advocate in your corner, someone who's not just looking to close a deal but to secure an outcome that truly serves your best interests. It means having confidence that every aspect of the negotiation has been carefully considered and strategically planned. And it means knowing that at the end of the process, you'll walk away not just with a successful transaction but with a positive experience that sets the stage for your next chapter.

As we move forward in your real estate journey, remember that with the right negotiation strategy, everyone can win. Whether you're buying your dream home or selling a cherished property, my CANVAS strategy and WIN-WIN-WIN approach ensure that we're not just participating in the market—we're shaping it to our advantage.

In the next chapter, we'll explore how these negotiation strategies fit into the larger picture of creating a community of clients and building relationships that last far beyond the closing table. Because in my world, a successful negotiation isn't just about one deal—it's about creating a lifetime of value for my clients.

Chapter Five

Beyond the Transaction

Creating a Community of Clients

When I first started in real estate, I thought my job was simple: help people buy and sell homes. But as I've grown in this profession, I've realized that what we do goes far beyond mere transactions. We're not just dealing in properties; we're shaping lives, building dreams, and fostering a sense of community that extends well beyond the closing table.

The Tapestry of Connection: Weaving Clients into a Community

Imagine, if you will, a beautiful tapestry. Each thread represents a client, and every transaction is a moment where that thread is woven into the larger picture. But here's the thing – in my world, we don't just tie off that thread and move on to the next. Instead, we keep weaving, creating intricate patterns of connection that grow more beautiful and complex over time.

This is what I call the Community of Clients approach. It's a philosophy that transforms the traditional agent-client relationship into something far more meaningful and enduring. Let me show you how this tapestry comes to life and, more importantly, how it benefits you.

The Olivetti Family's Journey: A Tale of Lasting Relationships

Meet Kyle and Sherri Olivetti. I first encountered them as nervous first-time homebuyers, expecting their first child and dreaming of a cozy nest to call their own. Little did they know that finding their starter home was just the beginning of our journey together.

After we found them the perfect two-bedroom bungalow, I made it a point to stay connected. Remembering Sherri's passion for gardening, I surprised her the following spring with heirloom tomato seedlings and some gardening tips. It wasn't about making another sale; it was about showing that I listened, I remembered, and I cared.

As their family grew, so did their needs. When Kyle received a promotion, I was there to guide them through selling their starter home and finding a larger one to accommodate their now family of four. But our relationship wasn't just about buying and selling houses.

I introduced the Olivetti's to other families in the Cardano Client Community through my bi-annual "Neighbor Movie Nights." These weren't stuffy networking events or sales pitches in disguise. They were fun, relaxed gatherings where past and current clients could meet, mingle, and form connections.

At one of these movie events, Sherri met Lisa, a pediatrician who had recently moved to the area. Not only did Sherri find a trusted doctor for her children, but she also gained a close friend. These kinds of connections happen all the time in our community, creating a web of relationships that enrich everyone's lives.

When the Olivetti's needed to renovate their kitchen, they didn't have to scramble through online reviews or take a chance on an unknown entity. They called me, and within hours, I had connected them with John, a master contractor I've worked with for years. John not only did an excellent job but also gave them a preferential rate as part of our network.

As the years passed, I was there to guide the Olivetti's through various life changes. When Sherri's parents needed to downsize, I helped them find the perfect retirement condo. When Kyle started a home-based business, I advised him on creating an ideal home office space that would add value to their property.

The Olivetti's became regulars at my educational workshops. These weren't just lectures; they were interactive sessions where clients could share their experiences, ask questions, and learn from each other as well as from expert speakers I brought in. At one energy efficiency seminar, Kyle shared how he had significantly reduced their energy bills, inspiring other attendees to make similar improvements.

Every year, the Olivetti's participated enthusiastically in our community events. There was our annual "Thanksgiving Pie Open House," where clients stop by for lunch, share news of their family endeavors, and pick up a large apple or pumpkin Pie for their Thanksgiving table. Then there was the spring "Curb Appeal Challenge," where clients competed to see who could make the biggest improvement to their home's exterior in a single weekend. The Olivetti's won one year, and they always participate in our Thanksgiving pie open house and bring friends. These events did more than just create fun memories. They fostered a sense of belonging and community that enriched everyone's lives.

Now, almost two decades after our first meeting, the Olivettis' oldest is heading to college. They called me, not just as their realtor but as a trusted friend, to discuss the best way to leverage their home equity for tuition. As we sat in their kitchen – the very one I had helped them renovate years ago – Sherri turned to me and said, "Diane, you're not just our realtor. You're part of our family. We couldn't imagine navigating all these life changes without you."

This is the kind of relationship I strive to build with every client. It's not about a single transaction; it's about creating a lifelong connection that adds value at every stage of your journey.

Creating a Legacy of Care: The Story of Glenside Gardens

Now, let me tell you about Glenside Gardens, a development that perfectly embodies my approach to client relationships and community building.

It started with the Millers, a young couple buying their first home. As we walked through a charming bungalow, I didn't just see a house – I saw the potential for a vibrant community. I shared my vision with the Millers, and they were excited to be part of it.

Over the next few years, I helped several other families find homes in Glenside Gardens. With each new client, I didn't just think about the immediate sale. I considered how they would fit into the growing community, how their needs might change over time, and how we could create lasting connections.

I engaged with the Glenside Gardens residents regularly, organizing block parties, yard sales, and neighborhood improvement projects. These weren't just social events – they were opportunities for neighbors to form genuine bonds and support systems.

Take the story of the Taylors and the Garcias. When the Taylors needed to sell quickly due to a job relocation, they were stressed about getting their home ready for market. That's when the Garcias, who I had also helped move to Glenside Gardens, stepped in. They offered to help with the move and house staging, turning a potentially stressful situation into a community effort. This spirit of mutual support became a hallmark of the street.

I made it a point to continuously educate the Glenside Gardens residents. We had workshops on everything from home maintenance to local market trends. When the city proposed a new development nearby, I organized a session to help residents understand the potential impact on their property values and quality of life. Knowledge is power, and I wanted my clients to feel empowered in all aspects of homeownership.

The results of this long-term, engaged approach were remarkable. Glenside Gardens became known as one of the most desirable developments in the area. Home values appreciated steadily, but more importantly, it was a place where neighbors became friends, where children grew up together, and where a sense of belonging flourished.

One story that always touches my heart is that of Mrs. Colagio, an elderly widow who moved to Glenside Gardens to be closer to her daughter. Initially, Mrs. Colagia was hesitant about the move and worried about feeling isolated in a new neighborhood. But within weeks, she was attending community potlucks, teaching her neighbors how to make dumplings, and finding companionship she never expected. Her daughter later told me, with tears in her eyes, "Mom's not just living near me now. She's living fully."

Twenty years after that first sale to the Millers, I stood at a Glenside Gardens community celebration. I watched as grandchildren played in the yards where their parents had once played. I saw neighbors who had supported each other through life's ups and downs, chatting and laughing together. And I realized that this – this thriving, connected community – was the true legacy of my work.

As Mrs. Miller, now a grandmother herself, hugged me, she said, "Diane, you didn't just sell us a house. You helped us build a home and a community. That's priceless."

This is what I mean when I talk about creating connections that enrich lives for years to come. It's not just about the houses we buy and sell – it's about the communities we create and nurture over time.

The Ripple Effect: How Our Community Approach Benefits You

You might be wondering, "This all sounds great, but how does it benefit me?" Let me paint you a picture of how our community-focused approach can transform your homeownership experience.

Imagine you've just moved into your new home. Instead of feeling like a stranger in a new neighborhood, you're invited to a welcome mixer where you meet other recent buyers and long-time residents. You connect with a neighbor who shares your passion for gardening and another who recommends a great local school for your kids.

A few months later, when you need a reliable plumber, you don't have to rely on anonymous online reviews. You call me, and I connect you with a trusted professional from our network who gives you priority service.

When you're considering a home improvement project, you attend one of our workshops and get expert advice on which upgrades will add the most value to your home. You also meet other homeowners who've done similar projects and can share their experiences.

As your family grows and your needs change, you have a trusted advisor to turn to. Whether you're thinking about refinancing, considering an investment property, or planning for retirement, I'm here to offer guidance and connect you with the right resources.

And it's not just about practical benefits. It's about being part of something bigger than yourself. It's about forming friendships that last a lifetime, creating memories at community events, and knowing that you're surrounded by a network of people who care.

This is the power of our Community of Clients approach. It transforms what could be a one-time transaction into a lifelong connection. It's about creating a community where clients become friends, neighbors support each other, and everyone has a trusted advisor to turn to for all things home-related.

Bringing It All Together: Your Place in Our Community

As we wrap up this exploration of how we go beyond the transaction, I want you to imagine yourself not just as a homeowner but as a valued member of a thriving community. A community where your realtor isn't just someone you worked with once but a trusted friend and advisor you can turn to at any time. Where your neighbors aren't just people who live nearby but friends you've met through shared experiences. Where you have access to a wealth of knowledge, resources, and support to help you make the most of your home and your life.

This is what our approach is all about. It's about creating an experience that doesn't end when you get your keys or sign your closing papers. It's about building relationships that last a lifetime, fostering connections that enrich your life, and creating a sense of belonging that turns a house into a true home.

When you work with me, you're not just getting a realtor. You're gaining entry into a vibrant, supportive community that will be there for you through all of life's transitions. You're becoming part of something bigger – a tapestry of connections that grows more beautiful and valuable with each passing year.

Welcome to our community. We're so glad you're here.

Chapter Six

Preparation Meets Opportunity

Starting the Home Sale Process Early

In the world of real estate, timing is everything. But what if I told you that the perfect timing isn't about catching a hot market or a seasonal swing? What if the secret to real estate success is in starting the process long before you're ready to list? This is the philosophy that has set my approach apart and helped countless clients achieve extraordinary results.

The Seed and the Harvest: Planting Success Years in Advance

Think of your home as a garden. Most people only start tending to it when they're ready to sell, frantically pruning and planting in hopes of a quick harvest. But I believe in a different approach. I help my clients plant the seeds of a successful sale years in advance, nurturing their property's potential overtime to ensure a bountiful harvest when the time comes.

This isn't just about maintenance or minor upgrades. It's about strategic planning and thoughtful improvements that align with market trends and buyer preferences. It's about transforming your home from a place you live to an investment you're actively growing.

The GARDEN Method: Cultivating Your Home's Potential

To help my clients understand this approach, I've developed what I call the **GARDEN Method:**

G - **Gauge market trends and buyer preferences**

A - **Assess your home's current condition and potential**

R - **Renovate strategically, focusing on high-impact improvements**

D - **Document changes and upgrades meticulously**

E - **Enhance curb appeal and interior aesthetics over time**

N - **Nurture your home's value with ongoing care and updates**

Let's dig into each of these elements and see how they benefit you as a homeowner and future seller.

Gauging the Market: Your Crystal Ball for Home Improvements

One of the unique services I offer is regular market analysis for my clients, even years before they're thinking of selling. This isn't just about tracking home prices. It's about understanding what features and amenities are becoming more desirable to buyers in your area.

For example, I noticed a trend in my market where home offices were becoming increasingly important to buyers. I advised my long-term clients to consider converting rarely-used formal dining rooms into functional home office spaces. Those who followed this advice saw significant returns when they eventually sold, as their homes met a crucial buyer need that many comparable properties lacked.

By staying ahead of market trends, we ensure that when you do decide to sell, your home isn't just ready for the market—it's exactly what buyers are looking for.

Assessing Your Home: The Blueprint for Improvement

Most homeowners have a blind spot when it comes to their own property. They either overestimate its appeal or fail to see its true potential. That's where my expertise comes in.

I offer my clients annual "home health check-ups." During these visits, we walk through the property together, identifying areas for improvement and potential selling points to enhance. This isn't about criticizing your home; it's about seeing it through the eyes of future buyers and planning accordingly.

One client had a unique sun room that they rarely used. During our annual assessment, I recognized its potential as a major selling point. We developed a plan to update the space, turning it into a stunning year-round entertainment area. When they sold three years later, this room became the focal point of the listing and a key factor in attracting multiple offers.

Renovating with Purpose: The Smart Way to Add Value

Home renovation shows have led many homeowners to believe that any improvement adds value. But the reality is more nuanced. Some renovations offer little return on investment, while others can significantly boost your home's appeal and value.

My approach is to guide clients toward strategic, market-aligned improvements. This might mean advising against a costly kitchen remodel in favor of updating bathrooms and improving energy efficiency. Or it could involve recommending a specific style of landscaping that's becoming increasingly popular in your neighborhood.

The Slow Burn Renovation Strategy

One strategy I often recommend is what I call the "Slow Burn Renovation." Instead of taking on large, disruptive projects all at once, we break improvements down into manageable, annual tasks. This approach has several benefits:

1. It spreads the cost of improvements over time, making them more financially manageable.

2. It allows you to enjoy the upgrades while you're still living in the home.

3. It keeps your home updated and in line with current trends rather than becoming dated all at once.

4. It reduces the stress and disruption often associated with major renovations.

I had a client who adopted this strategy, focusing on one area of their home each year for five years before selling. By the time they were ready to list, their entire home had been thoughtfully updated. The result? Their home sold for 15% above the initial estimate we had discussed five years earlier.

Documenting the Journey: Building a Home's Resume

One often overlooked aspect of preparing a home for sale is documenting its history. I encourage my clients to keep detailed records of all improvements, upgrades, and maintenance. This becomes invaluable when it's time to sell.

Think of it as building your home's resume. When buyers see a comprehensive list of improvements, complete with dates and costs, it instills confidence. It shows that the home has been well-cared for and that its systems and features are up-to-date.

I provide my clients with a digital "Home Journal" app that makes this documentation process easy and organized. When it comes time to list, we have a powerful tool that sets their home apart from the competition.

Enhancing Curb Appeal: The First Impression That Lasts

They say you never get a second chance to make a first impression, and this is especially true in real estate. Curb appeal isn't just about the week before you list; it's about cultivating an inviting exterior over the years.

I work with my clients to develop a long-term landscaping plan that matures beautifully over time. This might involve planting trees that will provide shade and character in five years or installing a low-maintenance perennial garden that becomes more lush and established each season.

One client took my advice to invest in professional landscaping design three years before selling. By the time they listed, their front yard had transformed into a magazine-worthy entrance. The impact was immediate—their home received multiple offers on the first day, with buyers specifically mentioning the beautiful landscaping in their offer letters.

Nurturing Your Investment: The Ongoing Care That Pays Off

The final element of the GARDEN method is perhaps the most important: ongoing care and maintenance. This isn't about major renovations or improvements. It's about the regular, sometimes mundane tasks that keep a home in top condition.

I provide my clients with customized home maintenance schedules, reminding them of important tasks like HVAC service, roof inspections, and exterior painting. This proactive approach prevents small issues from becoming major problems and ensures that when it's time to sell, the home is in peak condition.

The Ripple Effect: How Early Preparation Benefits You Now and Later

You might be wondering, "This all sounds great for when I'm ready to sell, but how does it benefit me now?" The beauty of this approach is that it creates a ripple effect of benefits that you'll enjoy long before you ever think of listing:

1. Enhanced Living Experience: By steadily improving your home, you get to enjoy a more beautiful, functional space right now.

2. Financial Planning: Spreading improvements over time allows for better budgeting and less financial stress.

3. Stress Reduction: When you eventually decide to sell, much of the work is already done, reducing the last-minute scramble.

4. Increased Home Equity: Consistent improvements often lead to steady increases in home value, building your equity over time.

5. Peace of Mind: Knowing your home is well-maintained and up-to-date provides a sense of security and pride.

The SECRET to Stress-Free Selling

To help my clients remember the key aspects of this early preparation approach, I've developed the **SECRET** acronym:

S - Start early, years before you plan to sell

E - Educate yourself on market trends and buyer preferences

C - Cultivate your home's potential through strategic improvements

R - Record all updates and maintenance meticulously

E - Enhance your home's appeal consistently over time

T - Time your sale perfectly, knowing you're fully prepared

By following this SECRET, you transform the often stressful process of selling a home into a smooth, confident experience. You're not rushing to get your home ready for the market; you're simply putting the finishing touches on years of thoughtful preparation.

From Proactive to Profitable: The Long-Term Value of Early Preparation

The true value of this approach becomes clear when it's time to sell. Homes that have been thoughtfully prepared over the years often:

1. Sell faster, reducing time on the market

2. Attract multiple offers, driving up the final sale price

3. Pass inspections with flying colors, reducing last-minute negotiations

4. Appeal to a wider range of buyers, increasing your pool of potential purchasers

5. Stand out in online listings, drawing more interested buyers to view in-person

I recently worked with a client who had followed this approach for seven years before deciding to sell. When we listed their home, it was the talk of the neighborhood. We received five offers in the first weekend, all over the asking price. The winning bid came in at 12% above our listed price, with minimal contingencies. The buyers later told us that they fell in love with the home the moment they saw the online listing and that the detailed home history we provided gave them the confidence to make a strong offer immediately.

Conclusion: Planting the Seeds of Your Future Success

As we wrap up this chapter, I want you to imagine two scenarios. In the first, you decide to sell your home and spend the next few months in a whirlwind of repairs, updates, and stress, hoping to get your property ready for the market. In the second, you decide to sell your home and realize that you've been preparing for this moment for years, with a house that's market-ready and a comprehensive history of improvements to showcase to buyers.

Which scenario would you prefer?

By embracing this proactive, long-term approach to home ownership and eventual sale, you're not just preparing for a future transaction. You're investing in your quality of life now, building equity steadily, and setting yourself up for a smoother, more profitable sale when the time comes.

Remember, in real estate, as in life, luck is what happens when preparation meets opportunity. By starting your preparation early, you're creating your own luck, cultivating a home that will be ready to shine the moment the right opportunity arrives.

In our next chapter, we'll explore how this preparation philosophy fits into the larger picture of creating a unique, "Diane-ize" experience for every client. Because in my world, real estate isn't just about transactions—it's about transformations.

Chapter Seven

The Diane-ize Experience

Unique Approaches to Exceed Expectations

When you step into the world of real estate with me, you're not just getting an agent; you're embarking on a Diane-ize adventure. It's a journey where every detail is tailored to your unique needs, where every challenge is met with innovative solutions, and where your dreams aren't just understood—they're amplified and brought to life.

The Orchestra of Excellence: Composing Your Perfect Real Estate Symphony

Imagine your real estate experience as a grand symphony. Most agents might play a single instrument, focusing on just one aspect of the process. But with the Diane-ize approach, you get a full orchestra, each element working in perfect harmony to create a masterpiece of service.

I'm not just the conductor; I'm the composer, arranger, and first-chair violinist all rolled into one. I've spent years fine-tuning this orchestra, ensuring that every note we play resonates with your specific needs and aspirations.

Let me tell you about the Johnsons, a family of five I worked with last year. They were selling their starter home and buying a larger property, all while juggling school schedules, work commitments, and a tight budget. It was like trying to compose a complex symphony with instruments that didn't always want to play together.

We started by synchronizing every aspect of their journey. I brought in my team of stagers to prepare their current home for sale while simultaneously scouting new properties that fit their growing family's needs. We timed the listing of their home to coincide with the spring market upswing, maximizing their selling potential.

Orchestrating Your Success: A Harmonious Approach

As we moved through the process, I played each instrument in our real estate orchestra with precision. When the Johnsons found their dream home but worried about selling their current property in time, I composed a symphony of solutions. We negotiated a contingency clause with the sellers of their new home while simultaneously creating a marketing blitz for their current property.

The result? Their current home sold in just five days, over the asking price, allowing them to move forward with the purchase of their new home seamlessly. But our symphony wasn't finished yet. I coordinated with movers, arranged for temporary storage, and even helped enroll their kids in their new school district.

This orchestrated approach turned what could have been a chaotic, stressful experience into a harmonious journey. The Johnsons didn't just buy and sell homes; they transitioned into a new phase of their lives with grace and excitement.

Yielding Maximum Value: The Power of Strategic Planning

In the Diane-ize experience, we don't just aim for good; we strategize for exceptional. This means looking beyond the immediate transaction to see the bigger picture of your real estate journey.

Consider the story of the Taylors, a young couple I worked with last summer. When they first came to me, they were looking for a starter home with a budget that seemed too tight for their desired neighborhood. But as we talked, I realized their long-term goals included starting a family and potentially working from home.

Instead of just finding them a nice first home, we searched for properties with the potential for future growth. We found a modest house in their dream neighborhood with an unfinished basement. I brought in a contractor friend who helped us envision how that space could be transformed into a home office or additional bedrooms down the line.

We negotiated a great price based on the home's current condition, and I connected the Taylors with a renovation loan specialist. Two years later, they finished the basement, adding significant value to their home and accommodating their growing family without having to move. This strategic approach to planning yields dividends far beyond the initial transaction.

Maximizing Opportunities: Innovation as Standard Practice

In the fast-paced world of real estate, opportunities can appear and vanish in the blink of an eye. That's why innovation isn't just a buzzword in my practice—it's a standard operating procedure.

Take the case of the historic Victorian we listed last year. Beautiful property, but it had been on the market for months with another agent. The problem? Younger buyers loved the character but were put off by the lack of modern amenities.

Instead of just lowering the price, we got creative. We partnered with a local tech company to create a virtual reality tour that showed the home with modern updates. Potential buyers could "see" an updated kitchen, a home office in the attic, and even a spa-like master bath.

This innovative approach not only sold the home but attracted multiple offers, ultimately closing 15% above the previous asking price. The sellers were thrilled, and the buyers got to put their own stamp on a piece of history. This is the power of maximizing opportunities through innovation.

Personalizing Every Interaction: Your Story, Our Focus

In a world of automated responses and one-size-fits-all solutions, the Diane-ize experience stands out for its deeply personal approach. I don't just learn about your real estate needs; I immerse myself in your story.

I remember working with Sarah, a recent widow who needed to downsize. This wasn't just a real estate transaction; it was a profound life transition. We didn't just rush into listing her home. Instead, we took time to go through her house together, room by room, as she shared memories and decided what to keep, what to pass on to family, and what to let go.

This process wasn't just about preparing the house for sale. It was about honoring Sarah's past while helping her step into her future. When we finally listed the home, it wasn't just a property on the market—it was a cherished space ready to be loved by a new family.

The result? We attracted buyers who appreciated the home's history and character. Sarah's home sold quickly, and she felt at peace with the transition. More importantly, she felt heard, understood, and supported throughout the entire process.

Harmonizing Goals with Reality: The Delicate Balance

One of the most crucial aspects of the Diane-ize experience is finding the sweet spot where your dreams align with market realities. It's a delicate balance, but when done right, it creates a harmony that resonates through every aspect of your real estate journey.

I once worked with a couple, the O'Briens, who had their hearts set on a specific neighborhood. The problem? Their budget was about 20% below the area's average home price. Instead of dismissing their dream or pushing them towards a financial stretch they weren't comfortable with, we got creative.

We expanded our search to include fixer-uppers in the neighborhood. We found a diamond in the rough—a foreclosure that needed work but had great bones. I brought in my network of contractors to give estimates and worked with a mortgage broker to secure a renovation loan, and suddenly, their dream home in their dream neighborhood was within reach.

Today, the O'Briens are living in their fully renovated dream home, with instant equity and a deep connection to their neighborhood. This approach of harmonizing goals with reality isn't about crushing dreams or settling for less. It's about finding innovative ways to make your aspirations a reality, even when the path isn't obvious at first glance.

Optimizing Your Property's Potential: The Alchemist's Touch

In the Diane-ized experience, we don't just sell properties—we transform them. Whether you're selling or buying, I bring an alchemist's touch to every home, seeing and unleashing its hidden potential.

Let me tell you about the Richards and their "ugly duckling" house. When they first showed me the property they wanted to sell, I could see why they were discouraged. The layout was awkward, and the decor was dated. But where they saw problems, I saw possibilities.

We didn't just declutter and slap on a fresh coat of paint. We reimagined the space. That awkward layout? We worked with a stager to show how it could be a unique, open-concept living area. The outdated kitchen? Instead of a costly remodel, we painted the cabinets, added new hardware, and installed a stunning backsplash—high-impact changes on a modest budget.

The result? A transformed home that sold in days, significantly above the asking price. The Richards were amazed at how their once-awkward house had become the belle of the neighborhood. This isn't just about cosmetic changes; it's about seeing the potential in every property and knowing exactly how to bring it to life.

Navigating Challenges: Grace Under Pressure

In real estate, as in life, challenges are inevitable. What sets the Diane-ize experience apart is how we navigate these challenges—with expertise, innovation, and unflappable grace.

I'll never forget the roller coaster ride with the Patels' home sale. Everything was going smoothly until the buyer's financing fell through two days before closing. Most agents might have thrown up their hands in defeat. Not me. I immediately sprang into action.

First, I reached out to my network of lenders to see if we could salvage the deal with alternative financing. Simultaneously, I contacted the second-highest bidder to see if they were still interested. Within 24 hours, we had two viable options: a new lender willing to fast-track the original buyer's loan and a back-up offer ready to go.

We ended up closing with the original buyers just one week later than planned. The Patels were amazed at how what could have been a disaster turned into a minor speed bump. This is the power of navigating challenges with expertise and grace—turning potential crises into opportunities to showcase our problem-solving prowess.

Yielding Exceptional Results: The Grand Finale

The true measure of the Diane-ize experience isn't just in the smooth process or the personal touch—it's in the exceptional results we achieve together. It's about exceeding expectations and creating outcomes that resonate long after the deal is done.

Consider the story of the Adlers, empty-nesters looking to downsize. When they first came to me, they were resigned to the idea that they'd have to compromise—either on location or home quality—to stay within their budget. But I saw an opportunity to think outside the box.

Instead of just looking at traditional single-family homes, we explored the idea of a luxury condo in their desired area. It was a type of property they hadn't considered, but as we toured options, they fell in love with the lifestyle it offered. Not only did they end up with a stunning home in their perfect location, but the amenities and low-maintenance living exceeded anything they had initially imagined.

The Adlers didn't just downsize; they upgraded their lifestyle. They now spend their free time enjoying the condo's rooftop garden and organizing community events in the shared spaces rather than maintaining a large house. This is what I mean by yielding exceptional results. It's not just about meeting expectations; it's about opening doors to possibilities you might never have considered and achieving outcomes that transform your life in wonderful, unexpected ways.

Elevating Every Experience: The Diane Promise

To ensure that every client receives this level of exceptional service, I've developed what I call the Diane Promise. It's not just a set of guidelines; it's a commitment to excellence that permeates every aspect of our work together.

Let me tell you about the Greens, a family I worked with recently. They were first-time homebuyers, nervous about the process and unsure of what they could afford. From our very first meeting, I made it my mission to exceed their expectations at every turn.

We didn't just look at houses within their initial budget. I introduced them to a financial advisor in my network who helped them optimize their finances, allowing them to comfortably afford more than they thought possible. When we found a home they loved, I didn't just submit a standard offer. I learned about the sellers' situation and crafted a proposal that met their needs while securing a great deal for the Greens.

Throughout the process, I created memorable moments for the family. When they were feeling overwhelmed, I surprised them with a picnic basket filled with local treats, suggesting they take a break and have a family picnic in the park of their potential new neighborhood. It was a small gesture, but it helped them reconnect with the excitement of their home-buying journey.

Even after closing, my commitment to their success continued. I helped them find the best local schools for their kids, connected them with trusted contractors for some minor renovations, and even organized a welcome party with their new neighbors. Six months later, when Mr. Green was unexpectedly laid off, I reached out to my network and helped him secure a new job opportunity.

This is what I mean by elevating every experience. It's about being more than just a real estate agent. It's about being a trusted advisor, a problem solver, and a friend. It's about creating an experience so remarkable, so above and beyond the ordinary, that you can't help but tell everyone about it.

Bringing It All Together: Your Diane-ize Symphony

As we wrap up this exploration of the Diane-ize experience, I want you to imagine your real estate journey as a grand symphony hall. Every element of your experience is carefully composed to bring out the best in your unique situation. Every interaction is performed with precision and passion.

And me? I'm your dedicated maestro, drawing on years of experience, a network of talented professionals, and an unwavering commitment to your success to conduct an experience that's harmonious, exhilarating, and ultimately transformative.

Whether you're buying your first home, selling a family property, or investing in real estate, the Diane-ize experience is designed to resonate with your specific needs and aspirations. It's about creating a journey that's as rewarding as the destination, a process that doesn't just meet your goals but expands your vision of what's possible.

In this symphony of real estate excellence, every element—from the first consultation to the final signature at closing and beyond—is carefully orchestrated to create a masterpiece of service. It's an experience where challenges become opportunities, where your dreams are not just understood but amplified, and where every interaction is infused with expertise, innovation, and genuine care.

As you embark on your next real estate adventure, remember that with the Diane-ize experience, you're not just getting an agent—you're gaining a passionate advocate, a creative problem-solver, and a dedicated partner in your success. Together, we'll compose a real estate symphony that's music to your ears and a testament to what's possible when expertise meets innovation and unwavering commitment.

Welcome to your Diane-ize experience. Let's make some beautiful music together.

Made in the USA
Middletown, DE
21 January 2025

69216562R00040